Original title:
A World Yet Dreamed

Copyright © 2025 Swan Charm
All rights reserved.

Author: Aron Pilviste
ISBN HARDBACK: 978-9908-1-4222-7
ISBN PAPERBACK: 978-9908-1-4223-4
ISBN EBOOK: 978-9908-1-4224-1

Whirls of Imagination Yet to Blossom

In fields where dreams take flight,
Colors swirl in pure delight.
Whispers dance in breezy air,
Hopes awaken everywhere.

The stars above begin to shine,
Guiding hearts with love divine.
Imagination starts to bloom,
Casting away the shadows' gloom.

A canvas waits for brush and hue,
Stories told, both old and new.
Each thought a petal, light and free,
Blossoming in harmony.

Through winding paths of endless might,
Visions twirl in radiant light.
In the garden of the mind,
Treasures hidden, yet to find.

With every step, we start to see,
A universe of possibility.
Whirls of dreams begin to soar,
In the heart, they yearn for more.

Pathways Leading to New Tomorrows

Upon the road where sunbeams gleam,
Hope whispers soft, like a quiet dream.
Each step ahead a brand new chance,
Life invites us to join the dance.

Through valleys low and mountains high,
We chase the wings of the morning sky.
With every path that we explore,
New horizons call us to their shore.

In twilight's glow, we leave behind,
The burdens carried, unconfined.
Together, hand in hand, we stride,
Towards the future's open wide.

Each moment carved like sculptor's art,
A masterpiece that warms the heart.
As dawn unfolds with colors bright,
We pave the way into the light.

The journey's sweet, though roads may twist,
In shadows cast, the sun persists.
Pathways leading, bold and true,
To the tomorrows waiting for you.

Where Canvas Meets the Infinite

Brush in hand, a dream takes flight,
Colors swirl in day and night.
A canvas blank, a world to see,
Where every stroke sets spirits free.

Beyond the limits, visions dance,
Each hue a story, each line a chance.
In every corner, emotions bloom,
Creating beauty, dispelling gloom.

Sails of Ambition in Uncharted Waters

A sturdy ship, the wind our friend,
With sails spread wide, our dreams ascend.
Into the depths of the unknown,
Where hope is sown, and courage grown.

The horizon calls, a siren's song,
In these vast seas, we all belong.
With every tide, our spirits rise,
Guided by stars in velvet skies.

The Symphony of What Awaits

Notes intertwine, a sweet refrain,
Whispers echo, banish pain.
In harmony, we find our place,
As dreams unfold, they leave a trace.

Each sound a promise, every chord,
Creating paths with every word.
Together we sing, the world in tune,
Beneath the watchful, silver moon.

Footprints on the Edge of Imagination

Step by step, we carve our way,
In realms where shadows twist and sway.
Each footprint marks a tale begun,
On this thin line, we are all one.

Waves of thought, like tides they rise,
With every dream, we touch the skies.
In whispers soft, the visions call,
Inviting us to break the wall.

Dreams that Dwell Beyond

In the hush of night they gleam,
Whispers float like fragile streams.
Bathed in silver, hopes ascend,
Woven threads that never end.

Stars awaken, dreams take flight,
Chasing shadows, clutching light.
In the depths where visions flow,
Mysteries of what we know.

Over mountains, through the mist,
Every heartbeat we resist.
Glimmers spark with every sigh,
In the dawn, we learn to fly.

The Palette of Infinite Visions

Colors blend like thoughts unfurled,
Swirls of fate in tender world.
Each hue whispers of the past,
A canvas where our dreams are cast.

Brushes dance with gentle grace,
Sketching love in time and space.
Every stroke, a silent song,
In this realm, we all belong.

Beyond the borders, shades collide,
A tapestry of hope and pride.
Imaginations dare to leap,
In this beauty, secrets keep.

Navigating the Uncharted

Sailing forth on seas unknown,
With the stars as guide, we've grown.
Waves of doubt may crash and churn,
Yet through the storm, our spirits burn.

Charts unmade and paths untold,
Every story waits to unfold.
With courage carved in every soul,
We find the strength to reach our goal.

Milestones gleam on distant shores,
Echoes call, while adventure roars.
In the heartbeats of the brave,
Lies the magic that we crave.

Paths Yet to Unfold

Footprints linger, tales unspun,
A journey waits for everyone.
Hidden roads that softly beckon,
Every twist, a new connection.

In the quiet, choices gleam,
Wounds can heal; we learn to dream.
Hands extended, futures bright,
Guiding us toward the light.

Moments slip through fingers fast,
Yet hope remains forever cast.
With every step, a promise made,
In every heart, the dreams won't fade.

Whispers of Tomorrow

In the quiet night, dreams take flight,
Stars above glimmer, shining bright.
Hope dances softly on the breeze,
Whispers of tomorrow, hearts at ease.

Future unfolds like petals in spring,
Every moment holds what life can bring.
Paths we choose, destiny's thread,
In the tapestry of words unsaid.

With each dawn, new chances arise,
Painted in hues of endless skies.
Embrace the warmth of coming light,
Whispers of tomorrow, pure and bright.

Echoes of Unseen Horizons

Beyond the hills where shadows play,
Lies a world unseen, far away.
Echoes linger, soft and clear,
Calling us forth with a voice we hear.

Mountains high and valleys low,
Guide our hearts where dreams can flow.
In the silence, whispers of fate,
Awake the spirit, before it's late.

Waves of time grace the shifting sand,
We reach for the stars, hand in hand.
A journey awaits, full of surprise,
Echoes of horizons that never die.

The Canvas of Possibilities

Upon a canvas, bright and wide,
Colors blend, a mystic guide.
Brushstrokes bold, dreams take form,
In the palette where hopes are born.

Each day a splash, a vibrant hue,
Crafting a life, sincere and true.
With every choice, the picture grows,
The canvas of possibilities flows.

Fading lines, yet new ones appear,
A masterpiece shaped by love and fear.
In this art, our stories unfold,
The canvas sings, both brave and bold.

Where Shadows Meet Dawn

In the hush before the break of day,
Shadows linger, slowly sway.
Whispers tease the edge of light,
Where shadows meet dawn, hearts take flight.

Gentle patterns dance on the ground,
In the silence, hope is found.
As the sun stretches its golden arms,
Darkness fades, revealing charms.

Artistry born from night's embrace,
Dawn awakens with a tender grace.
In this meeting, a promise is sworn,
Where shadows meet dawn, a new day is born.

Weaving through the Fabric of Time

Threads of moments intertwine,
In the loom where echoes shine,
Past and future dance as one,
In this tapestry begun.

Colors blend in vivid streams,
Whispers carried on the seams,
Silent stories softly told,
In each weave, a life unfolds.

From the dusk to breaking dawn,
Every stitch, a truth reborn,
Starlit paths that intertwine,
In this fabric, we align.

Time's embrace in gentle grace,
In the weave, we find our place,
History flows, both deep and wide,
In this quilt, our fates reside.

Threads of love, and pain combined,
In the weave, our hearts aligned,
Together on this vibrant ride,
Through the fabric, side by side.

Clouds of Untold Story

Whispers rise in skies above,
Veils of mist, a tale of love,
Wandering hearts in fleeting flight,
Painting dreams in shades of light.

In the hush of twilight's breath,
Echoes hint of life and death,
Clouds drift softly, secrets keep,
Every shadow, thoughts so deep.

Stars align in endless night,
Guiding souls with silver light,
In their glow, our hopes unspool,
Living dreams, the endless rule.

Carried by the winds of time,
Stories weave in whispered rhyme,
Clouds of wonder, skies so wide,
Holding dreams, we choose to glide.

Fleeting moments turn to air,
In the clouds, we cast our care,
A horizon yet to see,
In this flight, we find the free.

The Atelier of Future Dreams

In the workshop of the mind,
Visions flourish, intertwined,
Painted strokes of vibrant hue,
Crafting worlds from dreams anew.

Tools of thought, so sharp and bright,
Molding shadows into light,
Each creation tells a tale,
In this space, we will not fail.

From the canvas, colors leap,
Hidden hopes, we dare to keep,
In the atelier, hearts ignite,
Sculpting futures, bold and bright.

Fragments bright, a jigsaw pieced,
In the silence, dreams released,
Every brush, a path revealed,
In this realm, our fates are sealed.

From solemn thoughts to laughter's gleam,
In this workshop, we redeem,
Through creation's hands we soar,
In this dream, we seek for more.

Embracing Shadows of What Could Be

In the twilight's gentle haze,
Dreams emerge in softest ways,
Shadows whisper, futures gleam,
In their arms, we find our dream.

Walking paths of hope and doubt,
Voices echo, all about,
In the dark, we seek the light,
Holding shadows, bold in flight.

Every fear a step to take,
In the silence, feelings wake,
Embracing all that lies ahead,
In this journey, we are led.

Through the veil of might-have-been,
We find power from within,
Every choice, a thread we weave,
In the shadows, we believe.

With each dawn, the light expands,
In the shadows, our heart stands,
Together, we embrace the sea,
Of what was, and what could be.

The Lullaby of Tomorrow's Dawn

Whispers of night softly fade,
As stars begin to slip away.
The sun's warm embrace shall invade,
Awakening dreams of the day.

Birds chirp a sweet morning song,
Each note a promise to keep.
The world is waking, strong and long,
From gentle slumbers, deep sleep.

With colors bold, the sky ignites,
Golden hues dance on the rise.
Nature stirs with dazzling sights,
A canvas painted by the skies.

Children laugh in morning's glow,
Chasing shadows; hearts so free.
In this moment, let love flow,
Embrace the joy, let it be.

So hear the lullaby, so bright,
Of hope that dawn soon will bring.
Each heartbeat echoes pure delight,
In tomorrow's arms, we will sing.

Threads of Light in Twilit Gardens

In gardens where the shadows play,
Threads of light entwine, they dance.
Petals whisper secrets sway,
Underneath the moon's soft glance.

Crickets serenade the night,
As fireflies weave tales so grand.
Each flicker a twinkling light,
Guiding dreams through twilight's hand.

The blossoms bloom in soft array,
Painting dreams in fragrant hue.
In the stillness, spirits sway,
Finding solace in the new.

With every breath, the air grows sweet,
A tapestry of nature's grace.
Here, time and wonders gently meet,
In this enchanting, sacred space.

So linger in the twilight's glow,
In the peace of dusky lands.
Let your heart and spirit flow,
Through these gardens, hand in hands.

Reveries Adrift on a Celestial Sea

Drifting softly on a breeze,
Stars glimmer like dreams in flight.
Waves whisper secrets with ease,
In the realm of endless night.

Nebulas swirl in cosmic grace,
Painting tales of love and lore.
Time drifts like a slow embrace,
On this sea, we seek for more.

Galaxies twinkle in the dark,
Each twinkle a wish we hold dear.
With every ripple, we embark,
Chasing visions crystal clear.

The moonlight guides our serenade,
As constellations share their spark.
In this dance of light and shade,
We find the magic in the dark.

So let your heart set sail tonight,
On waves where stardust gently lies.
In the silence, find delights,
As reveries paint azure skies.

Beneath the Canvas of Possibility

Underneath a sky of dreams,
Where whispers form a bright exchange.
Imagination softly beams,
In colors vast and wide, so strange.

The stars become our guiding lights,
Each twinkle tells a tale untold.
In this space of wondrous sights,
New adventures soon unfold.

Brushstrokes of hope paint the night,
With every thought, a vision grows.
Underneath the shimmering light,
The heart ignites with boundless flows.

In the silence, courage thrives,
Within the palette of the vast.
We learn to dance with all our lives,
Embracing futures, dreams amassed.

So let us dream beneath the sky,
Forge our paths through fate's embrace.
In the realm where hopes can fly,
Explore the beauty, find our place.

The Lighthouse of Hopes

In the storm's embrace, it stands bright,
Guiding lost souls through endless night.
Its beam of promise, a warm embrace,
Whispers softly, 'You'll find your place.'

Tides may rise, the winds may howl,
Yet steady and strong, it bears the trial.
With every flicker, a prayer sent,
To those adrift, a heart's intent.

The waves may crash, the shadows creep,
But in our hearts, its light will keep.
A beacon for those who dare to dream,
Anchored in faith, a vibrant beam.

Through distant echoes of the past,
A testament that hope can last.
With every dawn, a chance to see,
The lighthouse shines, setting us free.

So when you wander, lost at sea,
Look for the light, and there you'll be.
Find solace in its steadfast glow,
For it is there your spirit will grow.

In the Realm of Unspoken Dreams

Whispers linger in twilight's kiss,
Silent wishes, a fleeting bliss.
In shadows cast by the fading light,
Dreams take flight, ready for night.

Upon soft clouds of muted hues,
Where hopes entwine like morning dew.
Every heartbeat, a secret shared,
In this realm, nothing is spared.

Voices linger just out of reach,
Lessons woven, they softly teach.
The stars above, a guiding song,
In the silence, we all belong.

With every breath, a wish takes flight,
Dancing softly in the twilight.
Mirrors of dreams reflect our fears,
Yet soothe our hearts with tender cheers.

So dare to dream, unbound and free,
In this realm, just you and me.
Embrace the night, let shadows gleam,
For nothing's ever lost in dreams.

A Journey to the Undefined

With every step, we leave behind,
The known comforts of the confined.
Venturing forth into the unknown,
A path uncharted, seeds have been sown.

In whispers of fate, we find our way,
Through twists and turns, both night and day.
With open hearts and eyes so wide,
We embrace the thrill of the undefined.

Mountains to climb, and rivers to cross,
In pursuit of dreams, nothing is lost.
Through the misty haze, we bravely tread,
The journey's song calls us ahead.

Each hardship faced, a lesson learned,
In the fires of courage, we brightly burned.
With every choice, we redefine,
The limits placed on a heart that shines.

So here's to those who seek with grace,
A journey forward to a new place.
In every heartbeat, every sigh,
We find ourselves, and dare to fly.

Shimmering Paths Ahead

As the sun will rise with golden rays,
New beginnings await, brightening days.
Paths that shimmer, calling our name,
With every step, we blossom and claim.

In gentle whispers of autumn's breath,
We leave behind shadows of death.
Every leaf a story, a song of the past,
Guiding us forward, so free and vast.

With dreams in our pockets, we journey on,
Through valleys low, to mountains high, we're drawn.
Chasing horizons, where wishes collide,
In the shimmering light, we'll ride the tide.

So take my hand, let's wander near,
Through every challenge, we'll show no fear.
For paths may twist, yet still they lead,
To places where souls are free to heed.

Embrace the journey, for it's our thread,
Weaving our futures where hearts are led.
In shimmering paths, we'll find our way,
Together, forever, come what may.

Silent Songs of Future Realms

In the quiet dusk, dreams take flight,
Whispers of stars in the velvet night.
Echoes of futures softly resound,
In the silence, our hopes are found.

Timeless journeys in shadows we weave,
Ancient wisdom of those who believe.
Notes of tomorrow softly entwine,
Silent songs in the cosmic design.

Hearts beating gently in the still air,
Carried by wishes, light as a prayer.
Faint melodies drift through the vast,
In this realm where all time is cast.

Glimmers of promise spark in the dark,
Guided by dreams' ethereal spark.
Lifting the veil of the yet to come,
Every whisper, a beat of the drum.

Together we wander through realms unknown,
In silence, the seeds of our futures are sown.
Each song a compass, leading us through,
To the future that waits, bright and true.

Unwritten Chapters of Existence

Pages unwritten, waiting to bloom,
Stories unfold in the vast, empty room.
Each heartbeat a pen, ready to write,
On the canvas of life, pure and bright.

In the margins, we find hidden tales,
Of dreams that floated on whispered gales.
Crafting the chapters of who we can be,
In the ink of our minds, we are wild and free.

Fragments of magic in every line penned,
Woven with care, fresh paths we'll send.
With every sunrise, a new page in sight,
Unwritten chapters ignite the night.

Pens poised in hands, inspiration ignites,
Across the horizons, we chase our delights.
Bound by no limits, no scripts to confine,
In the dance of existence, our spirits align.

Together we'll craft these stories anew,
With laughter and courage, our hearts break through.
Every chapter a step, every word a chance,
To unravel our truth in this grand, cosmic dance.

Illuminated Wishes

In twilight's embrace, wishes ignite,
Glowing softly, a beacon of light.
Captured in whispers, they twirl and sway,
Guiding our hearts, lighting the way.

Stars in the night share secrets untold,
Each shining glimmer a wish to behold.
With each breath taken, a spark is released,
Illuminated wishes, a banquet of peace.

Dreams woven bright in the fabric of fate,
Illuminated paths as we patiently wait.
Wanderers' hearts, entwined in the glow,
Embracing the magic in the dreams that we sow.

In moments of silence, they dance in the air,
Soft as the whispers of hope we all share.
Yet to be granted, they twinkle like stars,
Illuminated wishes, breaking our bars.

With every heartbeat, a wish takes its flight,
Awash in the glow of the deepening night.
Together we'll send our dreams up so high,
As illuminated wishes light up the sky.

Threads of Tomorrow's Tapestry

In twilight's loom, threads intertwine,
Colors of future in a vibrant design.
Each moment a stitch, each heartbeat a part,
Weaving the fabric from the depths of the heart.

Golden hopes shimmer through the dark,
Fleeting moments igniting a spark.
With patience and love, we carefully thread,
Tapestry woven, where dreams dare to spread.

In shadows we find the brightest of hues,
Tales of adventures, choices, and views.
Together we weave through the laughter and tears,
Threads of tomorrow dissolve in our fears.

Each strand a memory, a glimpse of our soul,
Crafted with care, it makes us feel whole.
In the heart of this tapestry, we'll find our way,
Through mysteries woven that daylight can't sway.

So hold tight the threads, let our stories entwine,
For the fabric of life is a journey divine.
As we stitch our tomorrows with courage and grace,
Threads of the future find their own place.

The Symphony of Undiscovered Paths

In the forest thick and deep,
Whispers of the shadows creep.
Each step leads to dreams anew,
A dance of heartbeats, strong and true.

Branches reach for skies above,
Echoes carry tales of love.
Footprints fade in timeless grace,
Nature's song, a warm embrace.

Sunlight filters through the green,
A tapestry of sights unseen.
Mysterious trails beg to be found,
In silence, magic all around.

Mossy stones and rustling leaves,
Clarity in what one believes.
Every turn, a story spun,
Unraveled threads where we begun.

Listen close, the secrets sing,
The symphony of wandering.
Paths unknown invite the soul,
In pursuit, we become whole.

Stars of Tomorrow's Light

Beneath the canvas of the night,
Dreams shimmer, bold and bright.
Each twinkle tells a story fair,
Of hopes and wishes in the air.

Galaxies whisper soft and low,
Promises of what we may sow.
Guided by the cosmic tide,
Stars remind us of the ride.

Constellations in their dance,
Invite us all to take a chance.
With every glance, we forge anew,
Boundless futures wait for you.

In the silence, fears subside,
We discover strength inside.
Together, we will chase the night,
With dreams as our guiding light.

Falling stars, a fleeting sign,
A moments thrill, a chance divine.
To reach beyond the skies so wide,
In unity, we shall abide.

Glimpses of a Hidden Horizon

Across the waves, the sun dips low,
A canvas painted, warm aglow.
With every tide, a secret waits,
Glimpses shared by whispered fates.

Mountains rise, their peaks unseen,
Inviting hearts to places keen.
The path ahead, a winding thread,
Leading where our dreams are spread.

Clouds like ships sail through the sky,
Carries wishes soaring high.
With every step, new wonders call,
The horizon beckons, urging all.

In quiet moments, truths reveal,
The tender visions that we feel.
Awake the senses, breathe it in,
To find the light that lies within.

Every glance unveils a choice,
Echoing within your voice.
The horizon waits with open arms,
A journey filled with subtle charms.

The Untraveled Journey

Each road unwalked, a tale untold,
Adventures waiting, brave and bold.
In the distance, echoes fade,
A dance of dreams, forever laid.

Footsteps linger, whispers call,
Maps unfold, inviting all.
Curiosity, an endless fire,
Takes the lead, fuels desire.

Stars align in perfect tune,
Guided by a silver moon.
Through valleys deep and mountains high,
In every moment, we shall fly.

The unknown beckons, fierce and bright,
Turning shadows into light.
Embrace the journey, fears must wane,
Each step forward just the same.

And when we reach the closing gate,
Reflect on all, both love and fate.
The untraveled paths, now clear and true,
In every heart, adventure grew.

Embers of Unkindled Fire

In shadows deep where silence lies,
The embers flicker, dimmed from skies.
A spark of hope, though faint it seems,
Awakens long-forgotten dreams.

Through weary nights, we search for light,
In whispers soft, we hold on tight.
The warmth of hearts that dare to feel,
A promise in the dark reveals.

With courage found in depths of time,
We stoke the flames of love sublime.
For every tear that falls like rain,
Transcends the past, ignites the gain.

So let us dance on fragile ground,
In unison, our souls are bound.
Together as the moments pass,
We rise to soar, we break the glass.

Embers of fire, we shall ignite,
With every breath, reclaim the light.
Our spirits soar, forever blessed,
In unkindled flames, we find our rest.

Lighthouses on Distant Shores

Amidst the waves, the lighthouses stand,
Beacons of hope on sea and sand.
Guiding the lost through tempest's rage,
They write their tales on time's old page.

Illuminating paths of dreams,
With every flash, the darkness beams.
A call to hearts that wander far,
To find their way, their guiding star.

The salty air brings whispered sighs,
As nature's voice through storms complies.
Each light a promise, strong and true,
That shores of solace wait for you.

Through quiet nights and sunlit days,
Their sturdy beams will clear the haze.
In every glance, a story told,
Of courage fierce and love so bold.

A symphony of waves and light,
They bless us all with endless flight.
Lighthouses shine, forevermore,
As guiding souls on distant shores.

Cradled in Tomorrow's Embrace

Beneath the stars, our dreams take flight,
In gentle whispers of the night.
Cradled soft in hope's warm chest,
Awaits the dawn, a sacred quest.

The sun will rise, a brand new hue,
In every shade, the world is new.
With every breath, we let love flow,
A tapestry of joy we sew.

The past may linger, shadows cast,
But each moment's gift dissolves the past.
In tender hands, our future lies,
Embraced by time, our spirits rise.

With open hearts, we forge ahead,
To chase the dreams, the love we shed.
For in the cradle of tomorrow,
We find a path through joy and sorrow.

So hold on tight, let go of fear,
In every heartbeat, love draws near.
Cradled close, together we stand,
In tomorrow's arms, we hold the land.

Dances with the Unseen

In twilight's glow, the spirits swirl,
In graceful arcs, they twirl and whirl.
With laughter soft, they weave through time,
A dance of shadows, rhythm, rhyme.

The unseen ones who know our names,
In echoes faint, they play their games.
Through whispered winds, their voices glide,
A longing force, where dreams reside.

Among the stars, they gently sway,
Beneath the moon's watchful gaze, they play.
A symphony of hearts that beat,
In hidden realms where spirits meet.

To dance with them is to believe,
That magic blooms when hearts conceive.
In mystic realms where shadows glean,
Life's greatest truths are often unseen.

So let us sway with souls set free,
In harmony, just you and me.
For in this dance, we find our place,
In every step, the unseen grace.

Shadows of Tomorrow

In the silence of the night,
Shadows dance with soft delight,
Caught between the past and now,
Dreams await, unspoken vow.

Echoes linger, stories told,
Paths not taken, glories bold,
Time's embrace, a gentle sigh,
The future waits beyond the sky.

Winds of change begin to stir,
Whispers speak, hearts start to blur,
Hope ignites in dusky hues,
Chasing light, we must choose.

Fleeting moments, shadows cast,
Threads of fate in twilight passed,
Together we will forge a line,
Into the dawn, our spirits shine.

Within the dark, a spark ignites,
Guiding dreams toward new heights,
Together moving, hand in hand,
In the light, we make our stand.

Whispers of Unwritten Horizons

Across the fields where silence breathes,
Whispers carry beneath the leaves,
Unwritten tales in every breeze,
Horizons stretch with gentle ease.

In the distance, visions rise,
Painted dreams beneath the skies,
Footsteps echo on untrodden ground,
A world awaits, yet to be found.

With every dawn, new paths unfurl,
Each moment a vibrant swirl,
Possibilities bloom like flowers,
Filling life with radiant hours.

Beneath the stars, our hopes take flight,
Guided by the silver light,
Every heartbeat, a story spun,
In the chase of what's to come.

Hand in hand, we tread the line,
Towards horizons yet to shine,
With courage, we embrace the light,
Together reaching for the height.

Echoes in the Land of Possibility

In the quiet glades, we roam,
Echoes whisper of a home,
Dreams entwined with thoughts profound,
In the land where doubts unbound.

Waves of chance crash on the shore,
Every heartbeat tends to soar,
In this space where shadows play,
Possibilities lead the way.

Fading fears like mist will clear,
Guided by a vision near,
Hands reached out to grasp the stars,
With every wish, the world is ours.

Stories woven through the night,
In the tapestry of light,
We are more than thoughts confined,
A vibrant future intertwined.

In every echo, dreams will grow,
To the rhythm of life, we flow,
Together stepping toward the grace,
In this journey, we find our place.

Visions Beneath the Starlit Mantle

Beneath the stars, our visions gleam,
Stories woven in a dream,
With every twinkling point of light,
Hope ignites the endless night.

In the quiet, thoughts cascade,
Whispers soft within the shade,
Every moment, an endless sea,
Charting paths to who we'll be.

Galaxies stretch across the skies,
Illuminating with our sighs,
Each heartbeat echoes in the dark,
Guiding us towards the spark.

Embracing mysteries to explore,
Unlocking every hidden door,
With the cosmos as our guide,
All our fears, we shall abide.

So, hand in hand, we reach above,
In the starlit realm of love,
Together crafting destinies,
While dancing with the gentlest breeze.

Stories Yet to Be Told

In shadows rich with unspoken dreams,
Each whisper holds a tale, it seems.
From ancient woods to the silent sea,
Every path holds what's yet to be.

Voices blend in the twilight's breath,
Echoes of life, of love, of death.
A tapestry woven, thread by thread,
Ink of the moments that linger unsaid.

Beneath the stars, they silently wait,
Hidden in hearts, they contemplate.
In the quiet, there's magic to find,
Stories unfolding, yet unconfined.

A child's laughter, a lover's sigh,
Time captures moments as they pass by.
Pages unwritten, a book still to fill,
Adventures await, as dreams distill.

The night holds secrets, precious and deep,
In every silence, the world is steep.
With ink and passion, the future is cast,
For every moment, a story amassed.

Vistas Beyond the Present

Mountains rise where the skies embrace,
Beyond the horizon, a new world to trace.
With every dawn, a canvas unfolds,
Vistas await, bright and bold.

Rivers flow with tales of old,
Carving paths, as life's stories told.
In every breeze, whispers of change,
Remind us that life is vast and strange.

Seas of azure, stretching afar,
Echo the dreams of every star.
The sun dips low, casting golden hue,
Inviting hearts to seek what is true.

Fields of lavender, scented and sweet,
Draw the wanderer, urging their feet.
With each step taken, horizons bend,
In vistas anew, our spirits ascend.

Future awaits on paths yet to walk,
In every shadowed alley, a spark.
Embrace the unknown, let your heart soar,
For beyond the present, there's so much more.

Dreams Tethered to Reality

In the quiet moments, dreams arise,
Beneath the weight of weary skies.
Tethered tight to hopes once lost,
Yet yearning for flight, despite the cost.

Whispers of promise dance on the air,
Eager souls reaching, hearts laid bare.
With every heartbeat, visions collide,
In the realm where fantasies bide.

A spark of courage, a flicker of light,
Guides the dreamers through the night.
Bound by the earth yet soaring above,
Dreams tethered close, wings of love.

Moments of doubt, clouds rolling in,
Holding our dreams like a solemn grin.
With every setback, we learn to stand,
In the dance of life, take fate by hand.

Embrace the struggle, the pain, the grace,
For every dream has its rightful place.
Tethered yet flying, we choose to be free,
In the dreamscape, just you and me.

The Flicker of Unsung Tomorrows

In the twilight glow, hopes start to fade,
Yet flickers of promise in shadows invade.
Unsung tomorrows, they whisper and call,
Embers of dreams that refuse to fall.

With every heartbeat, a story begins,
Carried by winds, where the future spins.
Eyes full of wonder, we gaze at the sky,
Searching for answers, wondering why.

In the quiet spaces, visions ignite,
Flickering softly, they light up the night.
Through the darkness, they choose to soar,
Unsung tomorrows behind every door.

Paths yet to walk, regrets left behind,
In the dance of time, our hearts intertwined.
Fleeting moments, stitched with gold thread,
Woven together, the dreams we've fed.

As dawn breaks softly, each promise awaits,
In the tapestry of life, where hope creates.
Embrace the flicker, let your heart grow,
For in unsung tomorrows, our spirits will glow.

The Diary of Future Dreams

In pages bound by golden threads,
A tale awaits, where silence treads.
Whispers of stars, soft as a sigh,
A longing heart learns how to fly.

Through ink and thoughts, I dare to chase,
Visions that time cannot erase.
Each word a seed, that finds its place,
To blossom bright in endless space.

Moments captured, the heart's own beat,
Drawn by the dawn's warm, tender heat.
Lifting hopes like wings on air,
Reflecting dreams that no one shares.

Beneath the moon's soft, silver glow,
I pen the stories yet to grow.
The future calls, a siren's muse,
In this diary, I cannot lose.

With each sunrise, new tales are spun,
In the canvas of life, we're all but one.
Chasing horizons, we strive and gleam,
Holding tight to our future dream.

Sketches Under the Void

In the quiet, shadows dance,
Colors mingle, lost in trance.
Each brushstroke tells a tale untold,
Beneath the stars, bright and bold.

Lines that twist, curves that bend,
In the dark, where dreams extend.
Textures whisper, secrets unfold,
As the hand moves, stories mold.

In the stillness, hearts beat loud,
Creating visions, hidden in shroud.
Muted shades, yet fiercely bright,
Sketches flourish, caught in night.

Through empty spaces, tales emerge,
In the void, where passions surge.
A canvas waits, open and wide,
For visions bold, to come alive.

Under the vast, eternal sky,
Imagination's wings will fly.
Every sketch, a piece of time,
In the void, our dreams will climb.

Notes from an Unfamiliar Dawn

Awakened by a song unknown,
The sun breaks through, bright and alone.
Each ray a promise, warm and clear,
Inviting whispers that we hear.

In shadows deep, the past will fade,
As morning light begins to invade.
With every note, the heart takes flight,
Towards the horizon, chasing light.

A gentle breeze carries my tune,
Guiding the way, a soft cocoon.
In every heartbeat, a new refrain,
Notes entwined in joy and pain.

Rustling leaves tell tales of change,
As the world moves, wild and strange.
Each moment a promise, fresh and warm,
In the dawn's beauty, we find our form.

Unfamiliar paths stretch out ahead,
With dreams to nourish, fears to shed.
Together we rise, unchained and free,
In notes of dawn, our symphony.

Flickering Hopes on the Breeze

Caught in the light, like fireflies,
Our hopes take flight towards the skies.
Each flicker tells a story rare,
Of dreams once lost, now bouncing where.

A summer breeze hums sweet and low,
Carrying whispers, soft as snow.
With every breath, we chase the glow,
Of flickering hopes that gently flow.

In twilight's embrace, shadows blend,
As we dance on paths that never end.
Every heartbeat sparks a flame,
With flickers bright, we'll stake our claim.

Through open fields, where grasses sway,
Hope weaves threads in the grand ballet.
We lift our eyes to the endless skies,
Flickering hopes as time flies by.

With every dawn, a new chance calls,
As night retreats and sunlight falls.
In the breeze that carries dreams anew,
Flickering hopes, forever true.

Unfolding the Fabric of Hope

Threads of light begin to weave,
In shadows where the lost believe.
Dreams are stitched with gentle care,
Hope awakens, breathes the air.

Fields of gold and skies of blue,
Every thought, a vision new.
In the heart, a spark ignites,
Guiding us through darkest nights.

Hands joined in a circle tight,
Mending souls with pure delight.
Promises like stars align,
In the fabric, love will shine.

Rustling leaves and rivers flow,
Nature whispers tales we know.
Every step, a journey's song,
Together we will all belong.

Through the storms and through the rain,
We will rise and break the chain.
Unfolding dreams, the fabric grows,
In every heart, the hope still glows.

Echoes from a Nuanced Future

Voices rise from distant lands,
Harmonies in gentle strands.
In the silence, truths emerge,
From the depths, our spirits surge.

Colors blend in vibrant hues,
Crafting paths we dare to choose.
Every echo tells a story,
Carving dreams in shared glory.

Windows open, visions clear,
Whispers of what's yet to steer.
Guiding lights, a beacon bright,
Leading us to brilliant heights.

Through the chaos, hope remains,
In the heart where love sustains.
Guided by the stars above,
We create, we heal, we love.

Building bridges, piece by piece,
Every promise brings release.
Echoing in timeless ways,
Future sings in brighter days.

Whispers of the Unsung

In shadows dance the tales untold,
Of quiet hearts and spirits bold.
Whispers weave through silent nights,
Carrying dreams on silver flights.

Each forgotten voice, a song,
In the depths where they belong.
Hidden gems in every soul,
Unseen stories make us whole.

Softly flows the river's grace,
Echoes linger in every place.
Through rusted chains and faded scars,
Hope emerges, reaching stars.

In the dusk, their voices hum,
A gentle rhythm, soft and numb.
Listen closely, heed the call,
For the unsung rise above all.

With each step, we honor past,
In our hearts, their spirits cast.
Together in this sacred breath,
We find life beyond the death.

Waves of Unknown Shores

Upon the waves, the whispers rise,
Secrets hidden in ocean sighs.
Braving tides and mighty swell,
We search for stories yet to tell.

Footprints washed by moonlit dreams,
Journeying through time's flowing streams.
Every ripple shares a tale,
Of distant lands and winds that wail.

In the tempest, courage grows,
Through the fear, our spirit glows.
Chasing horizons, hearts in flight,
Finding beauty in the night.

Waves will crash, and storms may roar,
Yet we'll brave each unknown shore.
Anchored firm, our hopes will steer,
Guided by the stars we clear.

Together, we will sail afar,
Finding peace beneath each star.
Every wave, a chance to soar,
Endless journeys, forever more.

The Unpainted Mural of Life

In colors bright, our stories weave,
Yet blank the space, where we believe.
With every choice, a stroke applied,
The canvas waits, where dreams reside.

Frayed edges whisper, tales unseen,
The brush of fate, in hands between.
A dash of hope, a splash of fear,
In silent hues, our lives appear.

Moments pass, like gentle rain,
Each drop a memory, joy or pain.
Together, colors blend and flow,
In this vast mural, we all grow.

So take a step, and paint your part,
With every beat, and every heart.
Though shadows linger, light will gleam,
On the unpainted mural of our dream.

Beyond the Reach of Time

In fleeting moments, seconds race,
Yet dreams linger in timeless space.
A whispered wish on twilight's breath,
Defying limits, even death.

Ticking clocks, they mark the way,
But heartbeats echo, come what may.
Through cosmic waves, we drift and glide,
In realms of thought, where we confide.

Eternal questions gently soar,
What lies ahead behind closed doors?
In every tear, a promise flows,
Of paths untraveled, love still grows.

So linger here, where time unwinds,
Between the stars, true peace we find.
In dreams that whisper, soft as rhyme,
We dance together, beyond all time.

The Magic of Unconceived Dreams

In shadows deep, where wishes dwell,
Unseen potential, casting a spell.
With every heartbeat, futures rise,
In silent spaces, truth defies.

The mind's canvas, blank and wide,
Painted visions, our hearts abide.
A flicker here, a spark untamed,
In dreams imagined, we are named.

So close your eyes, let visions bloom,
Awake the magic held in gloom.
For every doubt, a dream transcends,
In realms of hope, where darkness bends.

With whispered thoughts, we touch the sky,
Courage to leap, to dare, to fly.
In every heart, a dream concealed,
The magic waits, yet to be revealed.

Fluttering Pages of Tomorrow

In winds of change, pages turn,
Stories waiting, hearts to learn.
Every flutter, a chance to see,
The tale unspoken, yet to be.

With ink of hope, we write each line,
In life's narrative, we intertwine.
Through laughter's song and sorrow's tear,
Turn the page, embrace the year.

Moments like whispers, soft yet clear,
In every heartbeat, hold them near.
The future dances, bright and bold,
In golden tales yet to unfold.

So take a breath, and let it be,
In pages fluttering, wild and free.
To every ending, welcome dawn,
In the story of life, we are reborn.

Seeds of Tomorrow's Symphony

In the garden, dreams will grow,
Planted deep, where hope can flow.
Each tiny seed, a story told,
In whispers soft, their tales unfold.

Sunlight dances on their leaves,
In gentle sighs, the heart believes.
With raindrops' kiss, they rise anew,
A symphony in every hue.

Roots entwined beneath the earth,
Fostering dreams, giving birth.
Together strong, they reach for skies,
In harmony, the future lies.

Nature sings in vibrant tunes,
Beneath the watchful silver moons.
As seasons change, they push on through,
Creating life as they renew.

So plant your dreams, let them take flight,
In the dawn's embrace, chase the light.
For in each seed, a promise glows,
The seeds of joy, tomorrow sows.

Unraveled Mysteries of Fate

In shadows deep, secrets reside,
With whispers soft, they seek to hide.
Destiny's weave, a tapestry spun,
Twisting threads until they're one.

Each choice we make, a delicate thread,
A labyrinth where hope is led.
Through winding paths, our spirits roam,
In search of dreams that lead us home.

The heart knows well the hidden signs,
In silence, fate softly aligns.
With every step, a new path shows,
Through thickets thick and gentle blows.

As time unveils what lies ahead,
In quiet moments, words are said.
Embrace the chance, don't hesitate,
In the unraveling of our fate.

So heed the call, let courage guide,
Through uncharted seas, we must bide.
For life's a dance, an endless chase,
With mysteries framed in time and space.

The Horizon's Hidden Whisper

At dawn's first light, the world awakes,
With golden hues, the silence breaks.
The horizon calls with muted grace,
In quiet whispers, dreams embrace.

Waves upon waves, the whispers glide,
Carrying secrets from far and wide.
In pastel skies, the stories flow,
Of distant lands we long to know.

As shadows dance on grassy knolls,
The whispers weave through wandering souls.
Each breeze that passes speaks of time,
A lullaby, a soft chime.

So gaze beyond the setting sun,
And listen closely for the fun.
The hidden tales of night and day,
In every whisper, guided sway.

For in the calm of twilight's gleam,
Lies the essence of a dream.
The horizon speaks, if you know how,
To hear the truth in the here and now.

Dancing on the Edge of Thought

On the precipice where dreams collide,
Ideas swirl, in currents wide.
With every step, the mind takes flight,
In the world of shadows and light.

Thoughts like dancers weave and sway,
In endless rhythms, night and day.
Each twirl and leap, a moment seized,
Revealing truths that once were teased.

The edge of thought, a vibrant place,
Where visions spark and minds embrace.
With courage found in every risk,
We mold the air, with dreams, we whisk.

From leaps of faith, we learn to fly,
As wisdom blooms beneath the sky.
To dance with hope, to sway with doubt,
In the edges where ideas sprout.

So let your spirit take its chance,
And join the universal dance.
For on this edge, life's wonders gleam,
In every thought, a vivid dream.

The Dreamweaver's Tapestry

In twilight's embrace, threads entwine,
Whispers of night in patterns divine.
Colors collide in silence so deep,
Weaving the stories that shadows keep.

Glimmers of hope in fabric of dreams,
Starlit reflections in soft silver beams.
Each stitch a tale of desire's flight,
Captured in canvas, concealed from the light.

The loom of the mind spins tales yet told,
Adventures unfold as the night turns bold.
Figures in dance, like wishes set free,
In the dreamweaver's art, we long to be.

A tapestry rich with laughter and tears,
Threads colored bright with joy and fears.
In the stillness, where fantasies lay,
The dreamweaver whispers, guiding our way.

When dawn breaks the spell, the fabric will fade,
Yet echoes of night in our hearts are laid.
A new day emerges, the cycle renews,
In the tapestry's heart, we find our muse.

Beyond the Realm of Wakefulness

In shadows where visions silently creep,
Time bends and sways, bodies drift into sleep.
The mind sets sail on an ocean unknown,
Chasing the dreams in the twilight zone.

Whispers of worlds where the lost find their fate,
Linger on edges, through time they await.
Footprints in starlight, possibilities flare,
In the realm of the night, we learn to dare.

Beyond soft murmur of dawn's gentle rise,
Lies a place where the ordinary dies.
Echoes of magic in forms yet unseen,
Unveil the truth that whispers between.

Awakened by light, sensations collide,
Memories linger, where dreams often bide.
Each heartbeat a story, each breath a new flight,
Beyond the realm of wakefulness, we ignite.

So drift into dreams, where the wild thoughts roam,
In the dark tapestry we find our home.
Infinite journeys await with each night,
Embody the magic, feel the delight.

Seeds of Hope in Untold Landscapes

In gardens of longing, our spirits take root,
With whispers of growth, each moment acute.
Seeds of tomorrow are scattered with care,
Bearing the promise of love in the air.

Through valleys of trials, we wander and roam,
Cultivating strength, in this world, our home.
Each petal that falls is a moment we sow,
In untold landscapes, our dreams start to glow.

With patience, we nurture the fragile and small,
Their beauty reveals in the midst of it all.
When storms come to challenge, we stand side by side,
For hope is the sun, and we're hearts open wide.

From ashes of doubt, new life will emerge,
In the richest of soils, our passions converge.
Together we flourish, in shadows, we thrive,
With seeds of hope, we awaken alive.

Nature's embrace, a promise so dear,
In each budding blossom, our visions are clear.
Untold landscapes stretch, awaiting the light,
Seeds of our future, take flight into the night.

Murmurs of Forgotten Futures

In silence we gather, the past in our hands,
Murmurs of futures where the lost still stand.
Ripples of time in the currents of thought,
Echo through ages, the answers we sought.

Phantoms of dreams that we chose to ignore,
Cast shadows of wisdom on an ancient shore.
Each whisper a tale of what could have been,
In the chambers of mind, where echoes have been.

Forgotten visions in twilight's embrace,
Flicker like embers that time can't erase.
The stories unspoken, the roads left untried,
Hover like phantoms, in dusk they reside.

Soft calls from the future, remind us to seek,
The paths that diverged, the voices we speak.
In the labyrinth of choices, we wander in grace,
Murmurs of futures prepare the new space.

Remember the flickers of light in the past,
For dreams that were sewn have a grip that holds fast.
In the tapestry woven from futures we've known,
Awaken the promise, let seeds be sown.

Envisioning the Unseen

In shadows where the whispers play,
Dreams unfold and drift away.
A canvas blank, yet full of light,
The unseen calls into the night.

With every thought, a path we tread,
Through silent worlds where hope is fed.
Eyes wide shut, we start to see,
A tapestry of what could be.

The distant stars begin to gleam,
In darkened skies, we chase a dream.
Imagination knows no bounds,
In silent realms, our truth resounds.

Through waves of thought, we start to dive,
To seek the realms where dreams arrive.
An unseen dance, a gentle sway,
In the expanse, we find our way.

What lies beyond the cloaked embrace?
A world of wonders, time, and space.
Embrace the unknown, let it unfold,
In visions bright, our futures told.

Chronicles of the Possible

Upon the dawn of unturned pages,
Stories wait through endless stages.
Each word a dream, each line a chance,
To weave a world in vivid dance.

In whispered tones, the future calls,
Where endless growth and wonder sprawls.
Chronicles of paths yet untried,
Where every heartbeat, hope supplied.

From ashes rise, the seeds we throw,
In valleys green where spirits grow.
Possibilities spread wide as wings,
In tales of time, the heart still sings.

Solstice rays of golden hue,
Illuminate the paths we pursue.
In every twist, new stories born,
Guiding us from dusk till morn.

Awake the light where shadows dwell,
With every breath, a story to tell.
The chronicles weave a bright new fate,
In endless now, we celebrate.

Flickers of Unexplored Visions

In hidden corners of the mind,
Flickers dance, new paths to find.
A spark ignites, a whisper glows,
Unexplored visions that life bestows.

Through quiet thoughts like gentle streams,
We chase the shadows of our dreams.
Each flicker holds the promise bright,
Of realms unseen, a guiding light.

Layers of truth await, untold,
In fleeting moments, brave and bold.
With open hearts, we seek the flame,
To light the path, to know our name.

Bursts of color in night's embrace,
Illuminate the hidden space.
The unexplored beckons us near,
With every glance, the visions clear.

In sacred silence, magic grows,
In flickers bright, our spirit knows.
So let us wander through the haze,
In unexplored visions, set ablaze.

Tales Beneath the Stars

Beneath the stars, the stories weave,
In velvet night, we dare believe.
Each twinkle holds a tale or two,
Of love and loss, of old and new.

The moonlight casts a silver glow,
On whispered dreams that ebb and flow.
Forgotten paths and hidden trails,
Reveal the heart of ancient tales.

In every shadow, a truth resides,
Where mysteries and magic collide.
With open eyes, we start to see,
The beauty born from what will be.

A tapestry of hopes and fears,
In starlit nights, we peel the years.
The cosmos sings, the hearts align,
In tales of wonder, we intertwine.

So gather close, let stories soar,
Embrace the dreams that we explore.
Beneath the stars, we'll find our way,
In tales of night, forever stay.

Horizons Yet to Come

Beneath the sky so vast and wide,
We chase the dreams that softly glide.
The sun will rise with colors bold,
A tale of futures yet untold.

The waves will whisper secrets near,
Carrying hopes, dispelling fear.
With every step on unmarked ground,
New worlds await to be unbound.

Leaves rustle in the gentle breeze,
Painting visions among the trees.
Each flicker sparks a new embrace,
A dance of time in endless space.

In twilight's glow, we find our song,
The echoes of where we belong.
With hearts as sails, we are the brave,
Setting forth, we learn to crave.

Horizons stretch beyond our sight,
Yet in the dark, we find the light.
We'll venture forth, hand in hand,
To discover dreams on distant sand.

Imprints on Tomorrow's Sand

Footprints left by hopes so bright,
Carried softly through the night.
Each grain of sand, a memory's hold,
Stories waiting to be told.

Waves wash over, then retreat,
Clearing paths for dreams to meet.
With every tide that rolls away,
A dawn awaits with promise gray.

Children laugh, their joy a spark,
Filling hearts against the dark.
They write their wishes on the shore,
Imprints whispering, 'Seek for more.'

Beneath the stars, we cast our sights,
Navigating through endless nights.
One step at a time, we roam,
In every heart, we find a home.

The future beckons, clear and grand,
With dreams entwined in every strand.
Each breath a chance to start anew,
Imprints lead us to what is true.

The Lullaby of Forgotten Wishes

In shadows deep where dreams reside,
A lullaby flows, soft as the tide.
Whispers of hopes that slipped away,
Cradle the night, soothe the day.

Stars blink gently, hold their breath,
While echoes linger after death.
Every wish that once took flight,
Now dances softly in the night.

Forgotten songs in fading light,
Tell tales of yearning, hold on tight.
Each note, a promise held so dear,
In silence loud, they persevere.

In every shadow, a flicker glows,
Reminding hearts of what they know.
The moon will guide the lost and frail,
As dreams take shape in night's soft veil.

Awake to find the stars align,
Rekindling hopes, a grand design.
For every wish that dares to fade,
Will find a voice, unafraid, unmade.

Reaching for the Unknown

In the heart of night, we stand tall,
With courage as our guiding call.
Each step we take towards the void,
Unravels dreams we once destroyed.

With open arms, we face the dark,
Seeking truths that leave a mark.
The stars above, so far, so bright,
Hold secrets that invite our flight.

Beneath the veil of the unseen,
We dance with shadows, bold and keen.
The path unsure, yet we press on,
For in the doubt, new light is drawn.

Voices whisper from the deep,
Stirring dreams that long to leap.
We reach for that which lies ahead,
The thrill of what we have not bred.

So take my hand, we'll break the chain,
Embrace the wild, endure the pain.
Together we will find our way,
Reaching for the unknown each day.

In the Gardens of What Could Be

In the gardens where dreams sprout,
Whispers of hope quietly sing,
Petals unfurl, revealing the route,
To a world where joy takes wing.

Sunlight dances on emerald leaves,
Each ray a promise, softly glows,
With each breath, the heart believes,
In the magic that nature bestows.

Pathways twist through fragrant air,
Gentle breezes carry sweet scents,
Here in stillness, life feels fair,
And every moment softly relents.

Among the blooms, lost time returns,
Silence cradles the day's warm light,
As every heart in stillness yearns,
For the gardens of gentle night.

In the shadows where secrets wait,
Lives the beauty of what could be,
Let your spirit find its fate,
In the gardens, forever free.

Beyond the Veil of Night

Beneath a cloak of endless sky,
Stars shimmer like whispers of dreams,
In darkness where shadows lie,
Hope glows softly; it always seems.

The moon drapes silver on the land,
Guiding lost souls through the deep,
With a gentle, luminous hand,
Awakening thoughts from their sleep.

Each heartbeat echoes through the night,
A symphony of silent sighs,
In this vast, velvety flight,
Truth emerges as dark clouds rise.

Step past the fears that hold you tight,
Embrace the unknown, feel it flow,
For treasures dwell beyond the night,
In the dawn's light, let spirits grow.

Beyond the veil, where dreams take form,
A world awaits, steadfast and true,
Here, hearts brave the brewing storm,
And courage paints the skies anew.

Chasing the Unimagined

With every step upon this path,
We wander where few dare to tread,
Chasing echoes of our own wrath,
Into realms where spirits are fed.

Ideas spark like distant stars,
Lighting the corners of our minds,
Where possibility breaks the bars,
And the heart, to the unknown, binds.

Fear may linger, attempt to break,
But here we rise, unwavering, bold,
For every risk we dare to take,
Shapes the stories yet to be told.

In the dance of what's yet to come,
We leap through shadows, twist and twine,
For every silence, a distant drum,
Calls forth the magic so divine.

Chasing the unimagined ways,
Where the wildest dreams start to weave,
In the luminous shimmer of rays,
We ignite the fire and believe.

Wings of a New Dawn

As the night surrenders to light,
Soft whispers murmur in the morn,
Hope unfurls its wings in flight,
While the earth, anew, is reborn.

With a brush of colors so bright,
The sky awakens, blazing hue,
Each dawn a new chance to ignite,
A trail of dreams for us to pursue.

Birds take wing, flapping through air,
Their songs weave tales of what's to come,
In this moment, we banish despair,
Giving life to the heart's gentle drum.

The horizon stretches, wide and clear,
Infinite paths lie waiting still,
With each sunrise, we cast off fear,
And courage awakens our will.

Wings of a new dawn take flight,
Embracing the world with tender grace,
In the glow of the morning light,
Together we rise, finding our place.

Beyond the Edge of Dreams

In the quiet night, shadows play,
Whispers of hope drift away.
Stars beckon with a soft glow,
To places where wild wishes flow.

Beneath the veil of slumber deep,
Thoughts take flight, secrets keep.
Wanderlust stirs in the mind,
With visions of what we may find.

Dare to chase the light unknown,
In fields where the bold have grown.
Each heartbeat a step towards fate,
Beyond the edge, don't hesitate.

With every dream, a story sown,
A tapestry of worlds unshown.
Take my hand, let's float and glide,
Beyond the dreams where wonders hide.

Awake the spirit, let it soar,
Through realms where silence roars.
In the vibrant dusk's embrace,
Beyond the edge, we find our place.

The Unfolding Starry Canopy

Under the vast, expanding sky,
Stars weave tales, drifting high.
Each twinkle holds a secret bright,
Whispering dreams through the night.

Galaxies spin in gentle dance,
Inviting souls to take a chance.
Moments stretch like silken thread,
Where every wish can be fed.

Constellations form a guiding map,
Leading hearts that boldly tap.
A heartbeat echoes in the void,
Creativity and hope deployed.

Beneath this canopy so wide,
Starlit stories, dreams collide.
Each breath a journey, each sigh a star,
Reminding us how loved we are.

So gaze upon this cosmic sea,
And feel the magic set you free.
In the stillness, find your way,
Under the stars, let dreams stay.

Reflections on Invisible Paths

In the shadows where silence speaks,
Glimmers of truth, the spirit seeks.
Footsteps linger on unseen trails,
Where the heart whispers, it never fails.

Mirrored journeys, the soul's intent,
Each choice a moment, a message sent.
Paths may twist like a dancing flame,
In the echoes, we find our name.

Waves of time wash over the shore,
Seeking answers, yearning for more.
Moments unfold like petals in bloom,
Guiding us gently through the room.

Every heartbeat a note unwound,
In the quiet, wisdom found.
Invisible paths guide the wise,
Illuminating all hidden ties.

Listen closely, the whispers call,
In the stillness, you'll hear it all.
Reflections weave the stories told,
On invisible paths, we are bold.

The Poetry of Possibility

In every breath, a verse takes flight,
Words dance boldly, igniting the night.
The world unfolds in colors divine,
Creating magic, one heartbeat at a time.

Canvas stretching beyond the known,
Each stroke an echo, seeds are sown.
Imagination blooms in varied hue,
With whispers of what we can pursue.

Possibility flows like a river wide,
Carving new realms, where dreams reside.
In the silence, hear the call,
With every heartbeat, we can have it all.

Take a step into the light,
Embrace the spark that feels so right.
In the shadows, let courage rise,
In the poetry of possibility, we find our skies.

Each moment a stanza, each thought a rhyme,
Filling the pages, transcending time.
Together we wander, brave and free,
In the grand poem of what we can be.

The Unwritten Poetry of Existence

In shadows we linger, whispers unknown,
Beyond the horizon, seeds of thought sown.
Each heartbeat a verse, a silent refrain,
The ink of our lives, in joy and in pain.

The stars hold the secrets, silent and bright,
In dreams we unravel the threads of the night.
A tapestry woven with hopes and with fears,
Each moment a stanza that echoes through years.

Through laughter and sorrow, our stories unfold,
In the pages of time, the new and the old.
Let the world be our stage, the sky be our pen,
Writing the lines of our lives once again.

So gather your thoughts, let your spirit take flight,
In the silence of being, we find our true light.
The unwritten awaits, with magic untold,
In the heart of existence, let your dreams be bold.

Skylines of Untouched Dreams

Beneath the vast canvas, where dreams take their shape,
The skyline whispers of journeys escape.
Mountains high, valleys low, all beckon the brave,
With each step we take, our future we crave.

Glistening shadows in twilight's embrace,
A canvas of colors, the night shows its grace.
Each star a reminder of wishes once made,
In the tapestry woven, our hopes never fade.

Across the horizons, where the sunrise gleams,
We wander the pathways of our timeless dreams.
In the silence of dawn, let visions ignite,
A symphony plays in the soft morning light.

The skies are a promise, the heart an open door,
With every heartbeat, we yearn to explore.
Let the skyline unfold, a story so grand,
In the realm of our dreams, together we stand.

Stanzas of the Unexplored

In every corner of the world, there lies,
A whisper of wonders beneath open skies.
The stanzas of history, waiting to be told,
In the silence of nature, the brave hearts grow bold.

Through forests of mystery, know not what awaits,
Each path is a promise that opens the gates.
The rivers sing tales, the mountains recite,
In the poetry of life, we dance in the light.

With every step forward, new chapters appear,
The journey of souls, a story sincere.
Within the unexplored, treasures reside,
In the ink of our spirit, let passion be our guide.

For the stanzas we pen are the cries of our heart,
In the waves of existence, we all play a part.
So gather your courage, let your spirit soar,
In the pages of time, we are destined for more.

Flickers of Radiant Futures

In the glimmering dusk, where wishes alight,
Futures are painted with colors so bright.
Each flicker a promise, a dream still in flight,
In the heart of the moment, possibilities ignite.

Across tranquil waters, reflections of hope,
We navigate pathways, learning to cope.
With each gentle whisper, the future unfolds,
In the tapestry woven, our destinies hold.

Through shadows of doubt, the light starts to break,
Flickers of brilliance in choices we make.
Together we venture, hands linked in trust,
Turning visions to action, as dreams we must.

Let the warmth of tomorrow guide hearts through the dark,
With every small flicker, igniting a spark.
For in the dance of existence, we choose our own way,
In the light of our futures, we conquer the gray.

Reflections in a Kaleidoscopic Sky

Colors dance in the evening light,
Shadows twist in a playful flight.
Clouds weave stories up high above,
Mirrored dreams that we long to love.

Glistening hues of orange and blue,
Each glance holds a vision so true.
Nature whispers secrets to the breeze,
In this canvas where time seems to freeze.

Fractured patterns tell tales untold,
The sunset wraps the day in gold.
With every blink, a new scene's revealed,
In this wonder, our hearts are healed.

Underneath the vast radiant dome,
We find paths that lead us back home.
Hope ignites in the twilight's embrace,
As we journey through this magical space.

In the twilight, reflections remain,
Caught in the fibers of joy and pain.
We gather dreams like stars in the night,
In the kaleidoscope, we find our light.

Chasing the Flicker of Distant Dreams

In the stillness of night, whispers roam,
Dreams beckon softly, calling us home.
Flickers of hope dance far in the night,
Guiding our hearts to take joyful flight.

Through shadows we wander, embracing the dark,
Igniting our souls with a daring spark.
Chasing the echoes of futures unknown,
In the starry expanse, we're never alone.

Each step is a promise, each breath is a chance,
Caught in the rhythm of fate's wild dance.
We leap into the unknown with grace,
Finding our place in the vastness of space.

Fleeting moments weave through time's gentle thread,
Painting our journey in hues of red.
With eyes full of wonder, we reach for the sky,
Chasing the flicker where dreams never die.

As dawn breaks, we rise, with courage anew,
Echoes of dreams in every dew.
Now we embrace, come what may,
For in chasing the flicker, we find our way.

The Bridge Between What Is and What Could Be

Across the river where thoughts intertwine,
Lies a bridge crafted from hopes so divine.
Step lightly, dear heart, on the planks of time,
In this sacred space, we'll write our rhyme.

With each stride, the past gently fades,
While visions of futures begin their cascades.
What is, holds us, yet what could be glows,
In whispers of winds where possibility flows.

Hand in hand, let's traverse the unknown,
In the glow of the stars, seeds of dreams sown.
A heartbeat apart, we leap into light,
On the bridge, we embrace the perfect night.

Layers of heartache, yet layers of grace,
Within every struggle, we find our place.
Tales left untold weave through our song,
In this bridge of becoming, we both belong.

So breathe in the change with courage, be bold,
For the bridge we cross is made of pure gold.
Together we'll wander, forever we'll see,
The magic that lies in what could be.

Fantasies Cloaked in Morning Mist

As dawn unfolds with gentle embrace,
Dreams whisper softly, lost in this space.
Veils of the morning wrap secrets in gray,
Fantasies linger as night fades away.

Each droplet of dew holds stories untold,
Nature awakens with magic so bold.
Silhouettes soften in mist's tender hold,
Secrets of splendor begin to unfold.

In the hush of the morning, hope starts to rise,
Colorful visions paint the wide skies.
With each step, time dances in delicate sway,
Fantasies cloaked in the dawn's perfect play.

Awakened by light, we dance through the haze,
Finding our rhythm in soft, sunlit rays.
Touched by the magic, we learn to believe,
In the fantasies woven, our hearts can achieve.

So let us embrace the mists that surround,
In this quiet moment, true magic is found.
For every dawn brings a story brand new,
Fantasies alive in the morning's soft hue.